Dragonfly

Dragonfly

C.M. Clark

SOLUTION HOLE PRESS

SOLUTION HOLE PRESS

Copyright © 2016 by C.M. Clark
All rights reserved. This book or any portion thereof may not be reproduced or used in any manner whatsoever without the express written permission of the publisher except for the use of brief quotations in a book review or scholarly journal.
First Printing: 2016
ISBN: 978-0-996-7031-9-2
Solution Hole Press LLC.
www.solutionholepress.com

Cover illustration by J.L. Saury

Also by C.M. Clark

The Blue Hour
Three Stars Press, 2007

Pillow Talk, with painter Georges LeBar
Porky Pie Press, 2007

Charles Deering Forecasts the Weather & Other Poems
Solution Hole Press, 2012

Acknowledgments

"A Tale of Two Siblings" appeared in
Sunstruck Matches: Tigertail, A South Florida Poetry Annual
(Fall 2013).

"Amphibian" appeared as a broadside in the
2012 SWEAT Miami Project,
in collaboration with artist Dorothy Simpson Krause.

Dragonfly:
An Introduction

Poetry is the solution hole of literature: it purifies the language, filters text, distills meaning. As if decanting precious jewels, poets pour their words into the void, the vacuum of the ether, the solution hole of time, with the mighty hope that other souls who encounter them and sift through them will apprehend—and comprehend—the meaning of their poetry, the message they wish to convey not only to their own times, but to all the ages. That the message is liminal, subliminal or supraliminal matters not; it makes the adventure of *translatio studii* all the more exciting.

We drop to our knees and dig into the text. Perhaps we encounter a certain viscosity or opaqueness; this is to be expected when deciphering a foreign mind and a superior soul. Those who demand instant translucence and easy sense will be unnerved and rebuffed. But some of us remain, persevere, to sift through the words like the literary archaeologists that we are, to unearth the message and bring it into the light. We will not cave.

Such are we, the literary archaeologists who delve in the hidden and the cryptic, the treasure hunters who glean for messages from the past, who must dig for nuance and spade the words for interpretation, that we value the poetic expression above all others, for this art, above all others, encapsulates its message in beautiful and loaded language, heavy with imagery and connotation, pregnant with substance, rigged up with juxtapositions and metaphors bound to thrill the mind with novel impressions and distinctive imagination. Or so it is for successful poetry.

It's true that poetry has gone through stunning changes, forsaking cherished forms, such as the sonnet or the ode, shedding along the way meter and rhyme, even structural disposition of verses, "accidenting" language, making it collide, or telescoping it, or elongating it so that meaning careens from one verse to the next, or stops it suddenly, or catapults it across empty space between what used to be called stanzas. Games are played with its arrangement on the page, in startling ways, to create surprise, but also to aid in its interpretation. An explosion of words on the page creates an explosion of concepts in the mind; a current of words produces a flow of thoughts; a slicing of words chisels slivers of lacerated impressions. There are no rules, now, where poetry is concerned, no more caesuras, no iambic pentameter, not even conventional grammar. Rhyme ran out of time. Assonance might remain, but dissonance is just as good. Poetry has become dislocated from its traditions, from its moorings, and is free to roam, to flow, in new directions, into new dimensions. Its adventure is ours to follow.

An adventurous poet is C.M. Clark who, with the advent of her third book of poetry, entitled *Dragonfly*, just published by Solution Hole Press, continues her poetic exploits with vigor and with courage. She is truly, of all of us, the Keeper of Words, as one used to say Keeper of the Keys, who opens the doors for us and eases us into a world of her own making, where the dimension of time has been deconstructed and all three temporal elements, past, present and future, function simultaneously. The four seasons make their appearance, be it a jumbled one. (And only Spring deserves, sometimes, to begin with a Capital.) Place names pin the events down to a big continent, although Florida is present in all its sweat-inducing and insect-infested glory. Still, it's a Florida that receives a dusting of trans-Atlantic sand from the Sahara, to create hues of local color not seen in any recent past. It's a non-story of three females, Lissette, Jane, and Dead Helen, who, although they are certainly not jumbled, may be manifestations of one being, like what used to be called multiple personalities, in this case all vying for the attention of their Creator, the poet, Who turns from one to the other to inhabit their souls, to people her visions. Vision, along with blindness, its counterpart, is certainly the word to use, for the eye(s) is/are everywhere in *Dragonfly*: as a noun, as a verb; people's eyes, animals' eyes, hurricanes' eyes. The multi-faceted optics of the compound eyes of a dragonfly who enjoys 360-degrees vision is emblematic. But it's a dive-bombing insect who can also see ahead into the future and look back into the past.

Her own eyelids opening and closing, the poet's providential eye does not waver, and her stare is keen and resolute, even through her closed eyelids, when perhaps vision is keener, for it looks inwardly. She will have us see what she sees, even though it might fill us with an ineffable unease, a sort of recognition that her brooding poems mirror life. We are compelled to accept this conceptual version of life, along with death, its counterpart, as factual requisites, with everything else in-between. Twin bookends to frame her text.

Sisyphus had his rock; we have our solution hole. We dig because we must.

~Roy Luna
Miami, Florida. Spring 2016

For Anne & Laura

"While a Darner dragonfly can live for more than a year, relatively little of its life is spent as an adult. In fact, most of a dragonfly's life is spent underwater."

– Frank Whittemore
from *The Life Cycle of a Darner Dragonfly*

Contents

In Search of Serotonin 1

Light Diary 5

Meteorology 7

Archaeology 11

World's End 13

Prêt-à-Porter & Ready to Wear 17

Graffiti 19

Lamentations 21

Rimbaud Closes His White-Blue Eyes 23

Plight of a Middle-Aged Star 25

Rinse Cycle 29

Flesh & Bones 31

The Meringue 33

The Cat's Meow 35

Housekeeping 37

Stones in My Pocket 39

Traveling *Enceinte* 41

The Unveiling 43

To Market 45

A Tale of Two Siblings 47

After the Fall 49

Vegetable Stew 55

Jane's Lament	57
Scent of Skin	59
The Cutters	61
Equinox	63
Ignition	65
Sea of Reeds	67
Tap Dancing	69
December Sunrise & the Tubercular Vagrant	71
Coloratura	73
Interstate	75
Immigration	77
Clean	79
Helen Rising	81
Blanc and Blanc	83
Nuptials	85
Colorblind	87
Inheritance	89
Lissette in Mourning	91
Jane Preys	93
Amphibian	95
Drakes Becoming	97

Dragonfly

In Search of Serotonin

1. Gods' Beer

How did Jane fail

to feel the dragonflies launch
and cleave the air, the stun

that pries, the drone? There
will be no soft-petaled landing, no
honeyed tip to siphon-suck

the tawny nectars. Bedsores, sore
need, needles aside, she wonders what
can the rainforest eat, what color the eyes

that scan humming wings, blink
into being the mammalian letting down, her singular
sour flavoring of tardy summer. Blink

the dour sweat's residue sets
the heartbeat to uneasy diastole.
We once

called them darning needles, so sharp
and hook-pointed as to mend
a frayed man's sock, so

thumb-rubbed the threadbare heel. Somewhere
a quiver of larva kickstarts
the fuselage, guns

the ten thousand silicon wings. They sip
silently, fly blind. You better keep
your fever-burned lips to yourself sealed

and shut.

2. Vanilla

Like a queen, Dead Helen brings her creamy breasts
and a willingness to abdicate. How
could they know? They knew

to call it la petite mort. Something so visceral
hangs leftover in the sky, as all
exterior pulls away. Her focus

pristine, one rogue leg hair itinerant
to a fault, she wades thigh
deep, herself a half-tone on a grey-scale.

Big death, little
death what begins
with death? Deep brain

shallow breath
repurposed.

3. Soil of Eden

No surprise
the eyewall
is in your eyes, where the barrel drains

scoring one perfect circumference of there
and not there. There
in the absence of iris

twin dark suns dilate
and contract, bottomless
vestibules of rod and cone

circumnavigate palettes of human color, Lissette's
common brown, Lissette's
non-space of barely at bay

jackals. It's no surprise
the eyewall is
in your

eyes.

Dragonfly

Light Diary

It was the first day Dead Helen saw that light. The south sill
repaired, faced with granite, then

veined with lead pencil erasure. Not to mind the small gap
a putty-knife missed. She heard

the grind of gears, a revving engine. Someone was off going off,
someone else wore

the pretense of a fat afternoon, juicy with sun motes, random
dust. Yet the light

triangle isosceles promised
promised nothing.

When you ante up and plateau that one age, fall feels right, just fall just
right. Helen took time

being dead. Now here she is. Sigh off the weight of bird eyes, cat
stares. Just late summer

no need to excuse the lying the lying
down.

See what comes with the seed of old parents? Some fluke of kinked
    hardware
software corrupted. Not

the clear code bright eyes of newborns, with driving neck muscles, looking
up looking around for the young arms, fuller

breast milk-full of what fills the void. The seed of old parents scrambles
the code, eggs

with shells cracked, fragments of tired albumen tainting
the yolk.

No more honey light, sap from the honey tree, no more
winter carnivals up in years up

in the Ferris wheel before, before your light hair swallowed smoke
and carbon ash, unaware.

The short shift before dark. Apple candles and gale's pause, dark
waits its turn. Fall flattens,

light insinuates. How the leyline sours, abbreviates the sternum
    rupture. Light touch
fingertip smoothed over creped eyelid.

This is the time. Jane won't stomach an intermission. Play muse
play music. Relish the eulogies

measuring breakfast's renewable feast. Lost love, stay gone. Now's not
    the season
to re-flame cold-begotten Jane.

To add shine, Lissette mused, that was the algorithm behind the
    screen, the shattered
honeyed beer, the jazz, the gin & fizz of soft

pop. Silicon sand city, city rippling beyond abrupt brick – it's the shine
that sears the dead

end, the vacant lot vacant eyes of the vacant surfer boys, their
    light-blonde consorts
rehearsing misogynies

of a burned sun.

Meteorology

i.
There was a dream behind the market, behind the back alley of
strewn deliveries & leavings. The produce smell consigned and
discarded, greengrocer's grocery greens, sharp-string celery & the silk
of corn, tomatoes wounded, outer leaves of cabbage and lettuce. The
cat's roughage, local and

past prime. Poor corn.
Poor undone hairdo betraying
brute summer. Rift valley gone
rotten, pygmy corn,

poor corn. Stunted torsos and
game legs. Polio ears,
sloughed skin, such fair
sad silk. Everything you learned

you learned from the sweet corn and
the dust and the saffron. August
your school and your time
of journeyman. In the country

of August, silk fingers read breezes
for signs of one leaf's
beheading. Surprise
when shy yellow brighter

than blond peels back and husks
naked and sweet show. Dry
husks hang till stalks fall once
taller than the girls the boys eye

witness. It would be wrong to bring
your heavy heart to the sweet corn
protocols of cold beer and street food and hot
sun's savory air. But you know already you

already know.

ii.
Fall line and the push
somewhere in Osceola County, the landflow
fuses. It's hard to separate tall tales
from thick brush. Somewhere

the line hides. What is deciduous chained
to season's law, and everything south gears ever
green and flimsy, bent to winds prevailing. Lissette's view
faces southwest, where

where is the line angling compass rose where
the line between simulated fall and
fallen clouds,
spent fronds.

iii.
In the winter, Jane is invincible.
The evening sky, so serious so indigo so
how can anyone entertain frail

death, or the cells that mulch pandemic,
or a moment's indiscretion. Winter's spine
so stern and fierce, so

oblivious to skin rashes and limp
lost hair, lips
dry and sunk to gumline, so

where can she find the fading
evening, when night comes upon us
the blade-keen stab never

missing its mark, unquenchable
enthusiasm for birth
and withering.

iv.
Dead Helen hates
spring, especially spring
that comes too early with muscle torque

and brash buds in colors loved
by the living. For a girl with glasses,
she had a surprising talent – putting pets

down.

v.
Always of surprise and
its own share of Thanksgiving, the last
cold spells where invalids like to sleep
beneath the sun. Have no need

of nurses or homecaring women in white
with clean nails and island accents, or
aging parents who've lost their sense of smell, just
smells of pickling fish and wedding photos

mounted in clouded plastic. The cold
comes of its own will, a last
dark evening, canal water without
ripples, and roosting waterfowl

puffed along the shore,
but higher than the brackish black
higher
than the brooding banks.

vi.
Who was she, then, who
learned she could not sleep in
through the light, the swelling warm
swaths on the parquet. But

she could gift wasteful and thick inside the failing
muscles, watch him take on
demobilizing . Witness
teeth skewed and gleam, greeting

a vague acquaintance. In the marketplace, they
liked the bow-bent man, heels sliding, the breaking
the creased sides of bent shoes. Let him
drive with windows down

through the premature morning. Nothing
lost on the breath, a silent Ah! as the streets
slide horizontally along the driver's acute left elbow
bone pointing and naming the familiar. So

much faster than the impossible
shuffle, the only permission
given for those still upright
and vertical screaming toward ninety. The second

time erupted as if
flesh spoke, flesh given lips and tongue, as words
sluiced through a pastry cone, so sweet so
sticky sweet.

Archaeology

Dead Helen named her child Tree Sap, inside
floating Mesozoic root flies
and carnivorous gnats, bellies

torqued with blood.

Dragonfly

World's End

I.
There is pollen stenciling the air, pollen
or the smallest insect rioting, dying
in the long sun. Midsummer

is still weeks off. Yet
the heat of radiated leaves,
spent spears of lawn, still

dot a cloistered scene. Outside
fringes of roadside spearmint, a munioned window
tired and west-facing, animal, vegetable

or mineral all seem
the same. How tired the sun
must

be.

II.
It must be Jane's longest year. We measure
pulchritude in inches in degrees
north latitude. How many squinted sidewalk

stones does it take? The two wasps' nests done in
with quiet poison, tucked under the eaves, corpses black
blackhole and opalescent as the sun

passes. These

are the unremarkable totems that gauge limits.
I will wander back to the front lawn on the return,
the well. Wait with bucket empty,

wait.

Invisible fire grazing wire skinned of penny
insulation and hiding behind fleshy plaster, soft
and hard and

lacking clear level. Jane looked
and looked for flames,
smelled heat and the man shouts,

the hoarse alarms, rubber men relaying rubber
hose into the dark the darkened
hallways. We lived

next door.

The grandmother kneaded bread
unperturbed. Could
she see through the hand's move

the offhandedness, asking
for the jellyjar glass of water, to quench
a fictional thirst, ran

once out of eyeshot, earshot, who
would notice a small dirty blonde throw
water in the general direction

of all those
hot
bricks?

III.
Lissette is
Sacajawea's daughter, daughter
of that coy French furrier who skunked

out pelt and soft red skin. We who are not one
are all someone's daughter, riding the heaves
of rain. To reclaim

a marshland, a glacier's incipience, brackish
and stiff —refusing
to let land win

if
only for a time. Lissette
gives birth

and hauls that bundle
of cells and propensities
out to the headwaters

of Missouri country of waterfowl and great mammals, out
into the brooding acres
seeing if land will cede

to channel islands and passages of spice and silk. But land
but flesh must always
capitulate. What

was
Lissette
thinking?

IV.
In the beginning, Dead Helen drives to her mother's funeral, to
her son, when she wore
her greying hair Kentucky-long, to run

from the illness feasting
on her bones. Every mile
a torrid wrench, liminal victory

from its grip. What
was that trip
like? Cold portions

canned drinks. Feed
the corpus
human.

Dragonfly

Prêt-à-Porter & Ready to Wear

What does it mean
when the bougainvillea are
gone, when

all that brave magenta, peeled thin
skin gone. Those
wiry vines feast on dry

spring's dry climbing, but
the heat wears on
and the brave are gone. What

rouses Dead Helen from the beauty salon,
when the newborn lizards unstick
their feet, and brave vegans

turn down flies and slower ants
lingering and a-marching to no tune.
Dead Helen's perm wilts

in the weary air. Lizard
heads bob and
red glottis like strawberry pokes

and throbs, hungry for protein. Jane's neighbors
are home. The widower behind the silk
curtains, the red door, the boy

with lickable brawn and hungry eyes wandering, his wife
and infant daughter migrated somewhere
into west Texas to bed the iguana.

Dead Helen camouflaged,
she who witnesses
waits for something summer something

flowering.

Lissette's grandmother safety-
pinned her blouse
shut. It was an immigrant trick,
scorning stitches and the tailor

who charged too much. Such
is the predicament of yawning
cotton and shrunk flesh – the body turns
turns in on itself, turns a bare shoulder

a winged collarbone. She was less
than five, her sister not yet
born, not yet
fallen down the brick stairs, fractured her skull

not yet.

What if Dead Helen wasn't dead yet, chose
a manicure today? As cool
Asian fingers skilled

to sculpt and trim, rehearse the dance
the braille of digital luxe and prestidigitation,
Not-Yet-Dead-Helen muses

on the evening ahead, to wear what?
Something
right off

the rack?

Graffiti

Her roommate leaves her speechless
riding backwards through November, so
one day, Dead Helen finds

herself the crazy lady
ghosting along the naugahyde cars
inscribing nail-wedged cuneiform

her name, bracketed by "Carlos
loves —" and "— loves
Carlos…" and a penciled male member, surprisingly

lifelike.

Dragonfly

Lamentations

One.
While the babies doze, Lissette's
off-center, and the one duck limps around
on one lame leg. She thinks she

lamed him last fall, is
the one who skewered him from
the pool, landing him too rudely
on the dry deck, still young

with webbed stomp to chase
lamely after his brethren exiting,
the brethren, all a-limping. We
are all ducks with one lame leg. You

with the rogue blood reading, me
too web-locked to entertain
that calculus. Lissette numbers
her loved ones in pairs. Two arms,

two legs – one lame – two sons,
two cats, and one other,
the one who is always two, entwined
and twinned with me.

Two.
It began with a tick, the deep woods
woe. The poison metabolic, never
excretes, re-structures cellwalls, bloom-flow.

Jane always feverish, every afternoon, even
in summer, even
in deep snow. Lying
on the deep bear rug, deep

in the dry walls of old mountains.

Three.
Dead
Helen is social, well past prime, the party
in someone's scrimshaw kitchen, food

and flirty hors d'oeuvres
and decorator pillows, skirmishing perfumes.
The loudest guest, a hidden five-year-old
boy laughing behind his candied

hand. He saw her shift
some fabric sweat-wedged tight
from her jumpsuit's deep
fork.

Epilogue.
When dirty blondes wear pink
and one's shorter shirt over long sleeve is
violet, and one

lays her fogged hair
on the man's pliant hands, and one
strokes the woman's tweed cloth purse
clutched and shouldered off

at the next stop,
such as it is
when blondes twine
and twin.

Rimbaud Closes His White-Blue Eyes

Squinting past the spearmint,
fair country lane Jane might be far
from the girl next door, but the boy

next door has light white eyes, eyes
lighter than the twilight sky, and
she likes him,

too, even in summer months when
the slapdash breakwater can't cool
you. Late sun's drowsy lid sinks

shut in the Gulf, but
flirty shells last, litter the shore – me!
me! me! – innerskin's nude

abalone. Jane leers a while,
pockets one or two to
rehabilitate the castles

the condos of sand. When Jane lurked
these beaches years back, there was something
something else called sun

poison pocking your mauled skin starched after
afterburn and
irradiated tissue. Fever'd

bloom by night and
the chills and the sweats soaked
your beachfront sheets, supima

counted by threads and wet. Not even near night
nor new moon dark nor
blank before dawn

could parry the silk sick sheen. Toxin
leeching
rapacious

and unswerving, burning
the cancerous moles,
the virgin cells

alike.

They walk the walk in the evening, now
still summer so still
and breathless and air

salted with migrant African
dust. Like a repurposed pieta,
their perfected apex appointing

parents, the lucky dirty blonde and the boy
next door. In the dusk's heat, he abandons
gravity's premise and performs

the perfect circle, flipflops flying, summer shirt up
ended down, delineating perfect abdomen, yes
a perfect Leonardo wheel of arms legs hands

feet full fronting akimbo my window. Tense,
more plusperfect is Dead Helen wan with
woman's alto-voice, cartwheeling right

behind him.
Don't
deny forgettable her the perfect

cartwheel echoing her glamorous husband,
don't steal the haunt, sideswipe me, slay

my surprise.

Plight of a Middle-Aged Star

i.
Done
with the kitchen sink. Gin breath
over the sill's silt. Soap gone operatic,

extramarital, as clouds conspire to pin-arm
the sun. She anticipates when stealth
dark like sudden bankruptcy will come

come and claim everything. Towel-dried hair, actuarial,
depreciating sundown's glamour. Some say
ideal for seeding hormones, the surge

of air and serrated thirst, waiting
for warm night, bus rides
to the boy's neighborhood.

Homage to the unremarkable
undershirt, so sorry sallow and
laundered too

often, and in Jane's day,
boots. Even in summer. Relief
after the sun's swallowed

and swallows by turn ramshackle
twilight. Can't
wait until she can't

see. Can't see anything
beyond monotonous
branch-shiver.

ii.
South, the sun
hurries. Lissette can tell.
Through her west-lying doorjamb sees

someone young even younger.
Walks, steers
babies and expectant dogs

alert fur in the early evening. Lissette wishes,
blows out twice-bright candles
on stale cake, wishes

they
were still young, walking
late in the early evening.

Like devotees affianced
to raspberry candlelight,
her addictions lean towards earth's axis, tilted

slightly by imagined
degrees. Where
along the sun's path

do we ride?

iii.
The abandoned armoire has collapsed. Too much
sun, the distaste of exposure,
leaning angled to ground,

a sick sail. Where went the yardsale, the Lladró,
the jay-blue Wedgwood,
the clouded

decanter, dry of wine, so
invisible. Orange peels and incongruity.
Just a blond-wood chest along a sine curve

sinking into Dead Helen's blacktop.
Grim laminate,
tarpit

to crude core.

Dragonfly

Rinse Cycle

I. The Sudden Downpour

Yeah,
Dead Helen's last boyfriend would wash
before sex. Bar upon bar upon
plexiglas shelf, Irish Spring churned

the dust of the stop-and-go highway, the slow
pollen Swiss-dotting their afternoon
trysts. He swore

to relish her smell, could coax
perfume from deleting light
born to bleed and bell

the late last hours, and no one
showered all night and night showered
rain with blunted subtext.

II The Rushing Gutter

Outside
Jane's bungalow, wet vines mimed roped veins where
her midwife hands rehearsed
the washing of the dead. Nameless, someone

Jane knows. Someone without terror
to touch the lifeless skin, lift limp
arms wipe the sculpted

webs between fingers,
and scrub off the stink
of life. Such sour requirements,

residual bits only
half-swallowed. Why, when,
what matter rejoins the dark

tide, blind fires,
dispassionate soil. How
can the human the humus

disprove worms that dodge and
bite?

III   Down the Drain

With so little to go on,
Lissette masters baby-bathing, so baby's bath goes on and
on, washing the newborn flesh-meat
fresh from womb's cave, mother's muck still wedged

in just-emerged pores soaked
with pediatric sponge,
surgical emulsifiers to float away the gristle

of repurposed birth-string suddenly
discontinued, suddenly
keen and

redundant.

Flesh & Bones

Dead Helen's mother had beautiful legs, until
the day she died. Unlike most, the veins
stayed put, microcells

beneath non-existent hair follicle beds surging
still sufficiently to keep true blue
buried. It was mostly

on her birthday that the ringing of bone, the call
of bones loud and dancing their tango
below ground sounded

most telling. The tomato fields nearby
surged in lycopene and the red skin the seeds
insisting, liked the kinship

of all who pushed forward
in their time. Once-not-dead
Helen sought memory

before memory to think of the pelvic bones
that widened, seeking their most exuberant
effort. A child's still-soft

skull emerging as the bones and attendant
ligaments, muscle, tissues soon
pushed. Dead Helen called

out to her still-dead mother, the maternal
matter, the sharp strong bones that cradled
that skull, arm's length

to cradle the one
that now-Dead Helen is. Those smart femurs
straighten. Not shrunk

yet.

Dragonfly

The Meringue

No one can foretell the meringue, it
floats breathlike beyond the charging cerebellum. Adding
lemon only complicates things. A twist

a sharp suck of inner mouth. Jane's mother
the diabetic. Lemon meringue
her undoing.

Dragonfly

The Cat's Meow

Jane cuts her doll's hair, it
doesn't grow back. Moves on
to the long fake-fur eye
lashes, but horrified

stops after only one is
done. Poor doll. An open
and shut case, in
one eye only – the cat's

long pulled indoor
whiskers could not be far
behind. Only they don't grow back either or
so slowly, only the one-eyed bug-eyed doll

notices.

Dragonfly

Housekeeping

She believed her house unremarkable in November
a sundial of angles skewed
to catch the honey-hived swatches, to catch

the hourly chockmarks, cinderblock
inscribed. Jane never had
the homemaker's hand. No nose

for dust, the dinge along a cabinet's right-beveled
edge. But skilled in beveling
the afternoon, she weighed

in window ledges. Pulled knap
off armchair, feels four, four
thirty. As long

as light fluffed knobbed cotton, there'd be
still time still
time to pace the perimeter, remembering

how far a half acre moved barefoot. By five
the seats sink to armrest
to furniture that might as well

be sheeted for the season. A short
brown dusk. Wood,
fluting candles, apple scent

along dust motes, breeze
shifts hairs grey-gone-blond. All wind soft filters
blows grey by dark.

Dragonfly

Stones in My Pocket

It's time I walked
with stones in my pocket, walked
beside the dark spring, walked
sniffing out spearmint along the rockbed,
chewing, walking.

We never slipped that year, it never
rained that much.
It seemed grim to lay a grandmother down grim
to lay her down, like laying pocked copper piping lying
too long in the sun.

Swimming in the Merced's shadowless day
quick darts of nameless fish tattooing stroking
legs. Half Dome seemed
recently cracked, raw in striated levels
of punished rock.

Dragonfly

Traveling *Enceinte*

Slip. The mucus plug rearranged interior furniture.
Buffet and armoire changed places. Rugs hand loomed

turned. The featherbed creased a deep dent
where no body rolls no longer. No man's land

between coverlet and percale. She is waiting
for flood's time. Soon. Room to let.

Dragonfly

The Unveiling

Dead Helen remembers the Brown boys praying bedside
the grave of their father. Three sons in grey suits
in the heat of June, intoning the regret, the missed

burly push of a man with a small
moustache, greying at the lip's
corners, beneath

beneath the soil, the new shorn
grass, short cut and sparkling with chlorophyll. His grin
they carry, but not today. Jane roadside

sees no light of June sun
on teeth mouth. Somber sons' eyes and the bramble
of brows, intoning

regret in a language their pressed
trouser seams
won't unravel.

Dragonfly

To Market

Kathleen taught her how
to steam her asparagus. Use lemons
or lime, if necessary. The citrus

beloved by the neighbors kitty-corner
and across the canal. One year we canoed
to a party on the pool deck

on the lawn. Ah, suburbia. Siamese cats
and luck-starred tabbies
striped and co-signed, authored

in the town centers where strays
become gifts become lovers, later
when

the nest collapses and the lawn
urges forward meager shoots. The lawn
service kept to provide

consolation. Company
for Dead Helen on
Thursdays.

Dragonfly

A Tale of Two Siblings

In the creases of Spring
the big bellies
bloom. So

she sinks beneath the wheat, her chin
softened with chaff and flyaway dust. She
eyes the tired fields; the waiting

the wasting begins. Jane dreams of Nebraska, or
maybe it was Iowa or maybe
some other state with parallel parking

and forgettable area codes, football
teams jinxed with some animal
name. Jane

was no cheerleader, but she could thrash
and flail with the best of them, kick
her pleats as high

as the next girl. She was
the pretty one in high school. She
listens to hear

the seductive snare of the timpani.
The big bellies
bloom.

In Colorado they build them blue-eyed
and blonde
and blind. The glaze

of endless eastern-ridge snows
icing the fields, the wildflowers'
cornflowers' cool calm. Comes

glaucoma come Spring, and she
remembered the pond's crack
and hue of hyacinth bulbs, brisk on the breeze.

In the creases
of Spring, the big bellies bloomed, but
Dead Helen decides

to relocate, abandon
her date with death and date
a realtor in Park City, mix

with the powdered slope
crowd, ski sweaters without bodies
and those pricy shops on Main Street luring

like spicy Asian takeouts on the outskirts, so complete
the whiteout, so
only the shadows shine, only Spring will put a stop

to all that. In the creases
of Spring.

Why do married women dream of hotel rooms freshly made
up? Cold sheets,

towels folded like bleached animals, or
degenerate origami? They trust

the curtained light. They trust the hands folded like flowers, clean
of color, anointing

the migraine brow. The fire
that warms the corners, the fire

that refracts the crystal, the same fire
that soothed the cave terror, fire

chasing ravenous peccary, cooked
and smoked, felled mammoth, tender and rare, simply

well done. In the creases of Spring
the big bellies bloom.

Dragonfly

After the Fall

This reverie, this post
day – antediluvian. No cars
across the street, not

the battered wreck of a fender bender, not
the perched archer guarding the gate. Oh
look,

he has returned. How white
his hair has grown. Men
don't ply the same vanities

touch-up their roots. When
did this happen? When
did the sun make it past his eaves, when

did the season slip by
unnoticed? Already I mourn
the non-winter. Already

I remember scarf and gloves. When
will this favored sweetness return?
Light, too much light, oh light. Only

the young love the light. We
have a greater affinity
for shadow and

shadow.

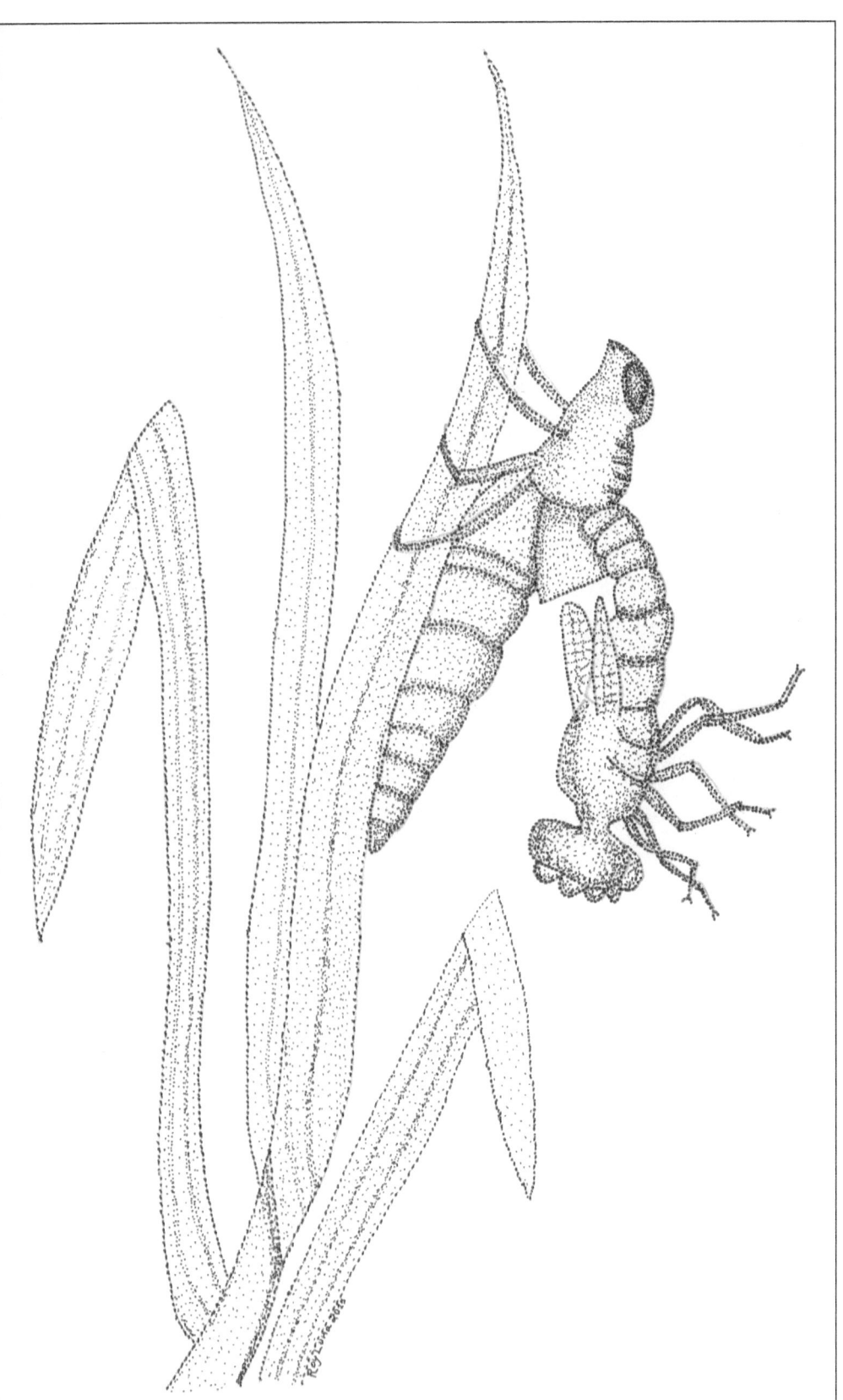

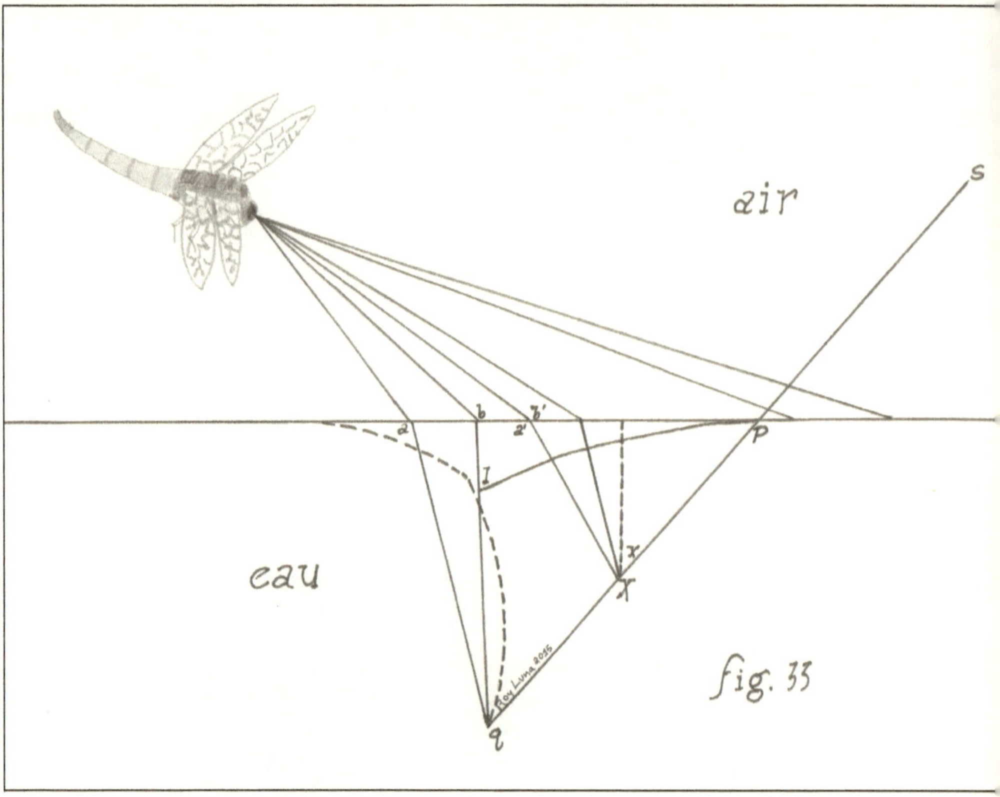

fig. 33

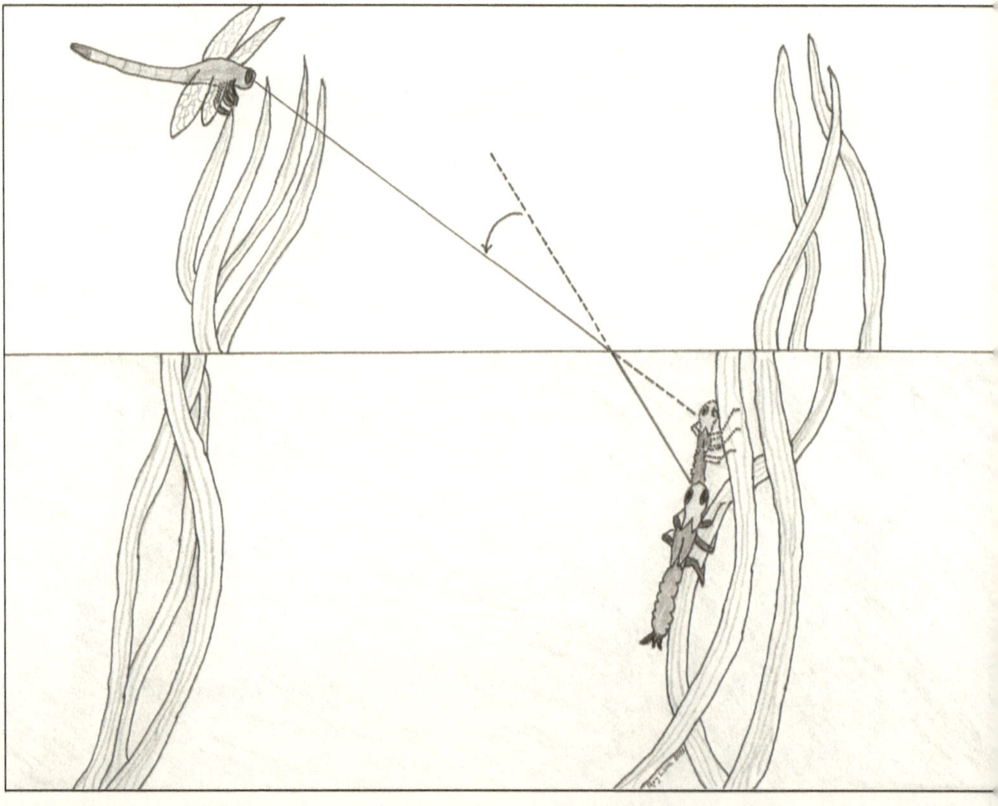

Dragonfly

Vegetable Stew

His two daughters, one
car alongside, at the side
where the housecleaner parks
set to, perpendicular and set

ready to garage. She
comes on Tuesdays, cooks
stew brings carrots, onions
he likes vidalias like

her mother. Only
on Sundays her sister shows
shows up a-glittering for brunch
off they go. Autumn

brings visits, bouquets
of tarnished leaves, slivers
of wheat, drowsing corn. Who
is hungry?

Dragonfly

Jane's Lament

I want to love
the fall, the urgent fade
color and light, what

in my heart wants
to love this dissipation?
I haven't much, and fall

has only its shored high
color, all soon
to dissolve in the fade

the fall. A late
bright surge, urgent
grasp of light, life

what color remains?
The skin
the skin

of leaves.

Dragonfly

Scent of Skin

Jane's father shot the dog
had to
shoot the dog, an old female

named Bonnie, alongside
the news of dead wife
succumbed to pancreas end, the

suffering's end. Shot
the dog, then
himself. In that

order.

Dragonfly

The Cutters

Dead Helen learned
to cut in college, learned
learned from Cathy
from Buffalo that
cigarette burns
on her freckled flesh
made everything bitter better.
(The boys who
made her knees weak
never gave Cathy the
time of day, but would
light her cigarettes. She never told
never told me she
never smoked.)

Dragonfly

Equinox

Spring is the time
for ladies. For Dead Helen
lifting her tired eyelids, her
drab braids, long languished

of the rush, the burnish. For
Jane, slender-fingered of the fingerpaint ensemble, bright
acrylics, sour oils cheek
to cheek with the canvas. Stretch. For

Lissette, as the babies turn
turn toward the stray
that lifts the boy
from womb to wardrobe

to tee-shirt and Hawaiian prints
on Bermudas. A wider world less
covetous than mother arms more droll
than cloying spring flowers. The irises

begin their bloom in Grandma's garden, dwarf
marigolds and the lilacs
the lilacs! Redolent
and the stuff addiction draws from. Spring

is a trying time. The rich profusion, all
too much, too much
too much for empty wombs,
dying ovaries. Too much

for those of us who remember, love Lladró figurines of girls and hens
love, for those
of us who forget urban gardens, forgot
love, love's plenty, love's

meager, disgruntled offering.

Dragonfly

Ignition

Jane's truck starts
rough. And the power
driven window when open only

rises slot-closed with
reluctance. It's barely
dawn. The street curves, a sideshow

of porchlights peripherally –
otherwise black
paved unseen. Only

an exhausted crescent hangs eastward, feral frown. Head-
lights, abuse-scarred and dulled
with use, but the beams work

work doggedly. Over the rising
incandescence strikes – offering
a road divides, coming

and going.
Which
to choose.

Dragonfly

Sea of Reeds

Lissette's kids stalled,
cats-eyed the light
suspiciously. So soon?

they wondered. So soon
after bath so soon
the shadows stretch

so quickly the bristle
on grass-head pretends
dew, then

gone to somber uneven
mulch. Packing crate matter might
as well be inorganic or

shredded board, such blunt
grey. The kids'
cats lick

the bristling fur, bed down
day, bed down the bull
rushes. Moses waiting

the Princess's cool touch.

Dragonfly

Tap Dancing

Autumn brings the harpsichord, the melody
that remembers her feet her
skipping shoes, and a sweet wind to encumber
the ease of harvest, the days when shoes

had sole. Single
line melody, maybe one
instrument, two
at most. Sun

down among clouds. Will
storms come
soon? Will
Jane

trust herself even
after the infidelities,
the vendettas, embraces
in the dark

with a different plug-in
flesh?

Dragonfly

December Sunrise & the Tubercular Vagrant

The perfect cough. Laced-creased phlegm
and productive. Loose
flesh shapes loose shirt

skin-worn – by someone else
first? – or just plucked
from the single-sided sofa

one-armed, covered loose,
a sheet to render throat's
anonymous clearing the

invisible.

Dragonfly

Coloratura

She followed in her mother's footsteps, footprints
on the radio. Steps of vocal frequencies
her localized timbre. Was

anyone listening?
The resemblance – echo
of inner ear.

Those straight-haired American girls, straight behind the bar
straight and tall trodding the duckboard, trodding
flat-wet the boards behind the footlights,

their silk stick hair tied up
behind their tall smiles. Jane remembers
before she sank, shrunk and curved, lank-

sided and forgetful. Which
topshelf brand
sells best?

Dragonfly

Interstate

i.
The boys in their world who hurt Jane changed Jane brought Jane to such disgruntlement – jawline pulled the left corner of your lip low, sheen slid your glasses down the nose bridge wet tightened the lipline sent a furtive footpath of salt shock down between the twin towers of shoulders jutting, was it love?

ii.
Through the windshield refracting its way toward vehicular privacies and furtive self-touched texts and loud mimes of pop hits and one half-stop flat, a face sleeping mirrors the woman in the western sun, saliva along the cheek, miles away from the miles lane-changes and road noise anxiety. Just the hum of well-balanced wheels and sharp tread, steel belting to hold the heat, the line straight, the drool along the headrest, the tinted window, was it yours?

Dragonfly

Immigration

If there's any good for Jane's good,
it's the god of cells the heaven
of mitosis and permeable membranes. Who

they were that suffered steerage out
of Marseilles, out
from a horsetrack of curved timber out

from a place deleted from remapped country, map
redrawn. Jane draws in
her feathered brows with blond pencil, who

were they, and did they shave their legs? On land
did they comb their long buns out, when
did they go grey?

Dragonfly

Clean

Lissette, young and cross-
legged on the twin bed, single, singularly
without a second self, virginal still

in the bleached linens her mother
washed washed washed.
Laundry day, everything sang

of spring flowers.

Dragonfly

Helen Rising

It was time. Now Dead
Helen felt her face pushed
against the fishbowl's
curved side pushed

up against the sheet
surface of waterline, curving
slightly as a trembling
meniscus. Almost there.

The archipelago of resentments
like a garden path of round
stones lining their way
toward the bright surface, the

bright air.

Dragonfly

Blanc and Blanc

The colors of white leech the pucker of strawberry
the blush under flesh and the blond veins high
on the cheekbones, the armpits – the white

chocolate on vanilla flawing the inner thighs,
dainty wrists, little bone limning tree limbs dividing
white from gardenia from albino rose petal.

Sea foam gone white curdled with blunt air, colliding
with sand talc bleached and tawny oxfords gone shoe leather
read cow flank gone whiter than white. White

on the skin, the unsunned dermis the unsung
virgin membrane, fruit unplucked, savory
uncolored, all light and the absence

of light. Too rich that café con leche that
tawny skin that
crème de cacao that

cinnamon candy. Bleach
me back, bleach me
whole, your sentimental ivory

key strokes stir parlor games, the afterbite
outdoing hydroquinone, the unremembered confections and
azelaic acid.

Dragonfly

Nuptials

Dead-or-alive Helen should
have claimed her calla lilies, waxed grails
for grim doubt, only later, snug

solid in pink foil, not like, not
unalike the larger queens that flaunt one questionable
virgin birth, her mother's

bridal handful. Why
did that fair farmhand scale
the child's cell-wall, thin haired. They

were at hide-and-seek and he hidden
in rough bunks sought,
ruined. The white bride's

rainy evening hid
where scores of night hawks rubbed
summer thunder. These

young buds so firm
in earth, now they stalk
and stalk and push skyward

in vengeance.

Dragonfly

Colorblind

Jane has a pleated blouse. Sings
on the bias and walkways like escalators emerging
and dissolving. Sometimes it is blue, on

days when airport carousels empty, no bags
astray, on others
green.

Dragonfly

Inheritance

Everyone hides
a jewel behind
their cellular walls. Lissette's

was a voice of honeybees
and silver bells. And silver falls
in an unmapped Amazon tidewater rising

with departing dark.

Dragonfly

Lissette in Mourning

They scent the graves with
fresh petals. The veins

of color and bee craving.
The ring was her mother's, gifted

years before the breath surfaced
from chlorine's night tang, and

after earth blunted your flaws, sheared
his loud taunt, his loud love. You

want this icon, this effigy? How
can it surround your new life. The awaiting?

She brings this the hundred miles,
the last look. She must

love you more. Her worm bones
would want this.

Dragonfly

Jane Preys

Half days, half life --
how long before the radioisotopes
fulfill their final protocol? Expire

with all that nuclear trotting come to still, fire
the last rogue particle from its teak, settle
and wait for afternoon's prior

commitment: shortest day's quick
pulse and the outbreath, ah --
compassionate dark.

Dragonfly

Amphibian

Only

one lizard skeleton trapped in the window casement. No sign
of the red membrane calling gnats
and hopeful females. She serves lunch.

Listless lettuce and sour vinaigrette. Someone
whispers knowingly, "Knowing bridge would help
with the locals..." And bowls of crushed ice

and cobweb bodices. Wound wicker
porch chairs to discourage the rot. Bleach
for the mildew, talc for the cleavage. Anything

to disguise the mulch,
the relentless and sulking air. They plan
to strangle the swamp. Grow sugar

or something. To know

you must go fifty miles in and into
the wet, where roadside waters bulge and the dry
coaxes waterbirds onto rockbeds.

And the bald cypress, the glib pond apples
impossibly green. In minutes, you'll dissolve,
and still the saw-tooth sedge makes camp,

weds the water. Even in my sleep
I finger the glades like waving foils of liquid Nebraska,
flat to flat horizon.

Waters waters waters unreadable.
Resistant to landmarks and mapmaking, yet skilled
to speak the Seminole's mockingbird tongue –

keening Pa-hay-okee.

Some mornings, the air eases, less
mean, clawing the skin less, less
yawning the ghost orchids, less

gape-jawed. All jaw, it seems the gators sun
circling their moist nest, and crinoline airplants
curtsy, output oxygen. No letup though, so clothes cling

like worn water.

Ladies who must perspire, do. And so
ruin the starched shirtwaist
the self-righteous pintucks.

And so ruing, breach
the one cold truth,
the one wet drop of one woman's

wild sweat.

Drakes Becoming

The dangerous time, the spring, the males
attack one another's underbelly. Bloating
saliva, supremacy. The feathers

fly and float beyond the bank the brackish
water. The awful day
of the drakes. The day

that the fowl blood flies, and the females float
downriver without so much as one brush back
and over the pinstripe curve, the fragile

neck.

The Optics of Poetry
[Plate Illustrations & Commentary by Roy Luna]

The eye is omnipresent in *Dragonfly*. It is far more than just one poet's vision, for as she peers into her world of visions we the readers discern many eyes that stare back.

It was the first day Dead Helen saw that light.

We glimpse figures in the text who see, but also those who don't, like the *vacant eyes of the vacant surfer boys*, or *Jane roadside/sees no light of June sun*, or even better *In Colorado they build them blue-eyed/and blonde/and blind*. Rimbaud himself closes his eyes to the world outside, perhaps a defense mechanism in order to discern inner space more clearly. While the hurricane's eye careens blindly about, another set of eyes tries to capture the blur of hummingbird wings. There is sight, and color, here, so the retinal rods and cones come into play, the first to capture the light, the other to detect chromaticity.

twin dark suns dilate
and contract, bottomless
vestibules of rod and cone

circumnavigate palettes of human color [...]

Objects shine, but smoke and dust occlude; we see, but parts of this world are hidden from us, so we need to implement full use of our inner vision. The best metaphor of this vision is the dragonfly itself. Before its metamorphosis the nymph lives below the surface of the water, in a dark and murky world. Once it leaves its exuviae it is destined to live in air. Its vision must therefore allow it to compensate for refraction as well as having the precision to go after prey. The optics of the dragonfly must of necessity be complex, and so, too, must ours. We need to see past the refraction caused by the differing densities at the borderline of world and text. We need to seize the meaning on the fly, grasp its opaque beauty, apprehend its dark message, and see—see!—what changes in us. Metamorphosis is not just for the dragonfly.

Light, too much light, oh light. Only

the young love the light. We
have greater affinity
for shadow and

shadow.

C.M. Clark's poetry has appeared nationally in *Metonym Literary Journal, The Lindenwood Review, Dogwood: A Journal of Poetry & Prose, Painted Bride Quarterly* and *Gulf Stream* magazine, as well as the 10th Anniversary *Tigertail Anthology* of South Florida writers (Fall 2013). New work will soon be appearing in the upcoming edition of *Travellin' Mama*. Previously, Clark participated in programs featuring contemporary American poets at the Miami Book Fair International. She also served as inaugural Poet-in-Residence at the Deering Estate's Artists Village in Miami, resulting in the collection, *Charles Deering Forecasts the Weather & Other Poems* (Solution Hole Press, 2012). Prior collections include *The Blue Hour* (Three Stars Press, 2007), and the artbook *Pillowtalk,* with painter Georges LeBar. Clark has a Ph.D. in English from the University of Miami, and teaches writing and literature at Miami Dade College.

www.ingramcontent.com/pod-product-compliance
Lightning Source LLC
Chambersburg PA
CBHW020619300426
44113CB00007B/707